Om Chanting
and
Meditation

A way to health and happiness

Om Chanting and Meditation

A way to health and happiness

Amit Ray, PhD

ILP

Inner Light Publishers

www.inner-light-in.com

Published
by

INNER LIGHT PUBLISHERS
Rishikesh, India
www.inner-light-in.com

First Published 2010
Reprinted 2013

ISBN: 978-8191026931

Email: innerlight.in@gmail.com

Disclaimer: The theory and the practices discussed in this book are for general information. If you have recently experienced mental or emotional problems or are taking medication, you should seek professional medical advice or expert guidance before practicing meditation on your own. The author and the publisher accept no responsibility for any harm caused by or to anyone as a result of misuse of these practices.

To the Divine Cosmic Self 'Om',
who dwells within us all.

May this book guide and help all
who read it and spur them
on their journey to enlightenment!

Contents

PART – II OM AND LIFESTYLE

PART – III OM MEDITATION

PART – IV OM IN SCRIPTURES

Introduction

From the ancient Vedic period to the modern age volumes has been written about the glory of Om. However, the sincere seeker knows that none of those documents is sufficient to explain the beauty and the grandeur of Om. Words can not explain its majesty.

This book is my humble worship to Om. This work is intended to give more emphasis on the way to develop the subtle feelings that can lead you towards the heart of Om, the deepest silence and peace.

Om is not just a sound or vibration. It is not just a symbol. It is the entire cosmos, whatever we can see, touch, hear and feel. Moreover, it is all that is within our perception and all that is beyond our perception. It is the core of our very existence. If you think of Om only as a sound, a technique or a symbol of the Divine, you will miss it altogether. You have to approach it with an attitude of surrender and reverence. Surrendering, merging and dissolving in to the ocean of bliss is the key to Om chanting and meditation.

As you, practice Om chanting and meditation correctly, people will notice changes in you, as you may be looking younger, happier, energetic and also calm and poised. A long-lasting sense of well- being and balance will quickly manifest in your life. You will also observe a sense of joyfulness entering your life along with an ability to appreciate the many gifts that surround you.

This practice improves both, the physical vitality and the spiritual strength. Om chanting and meditation is to be practiced in an effortless, gentle and relaxed manner, full of joy, enthusiasm and love. However, if you feel any conspicuous physical or mental discomfort during any meditation, discontinue the practice and take expert advice.

Contrary to the popular belief, Om chanting and Om meditation is not a sacred right exclusively reserved for the religious ascetics and mendicants. Neither it is a privilege preserved for the spiritually advanced souls, nor it is necessary to subscribe to a particular belief system for undertaking the practice of Om chanting and Om meditation. This is a practice of universal nature, which anyone with a reasonably healthy body and mind can undertake for peace, health and relaxation. Om chanting and meditation has been used by the seekers from countless centuries for a more rich and fulfilling experience of life.

You are a cosmic flower. Om chanting is the process of opening the petals of that psychic flower. It is a very tender, loving, delicate, soft and gradual process of opening the hidden dimensions of highest human potential. There is no hurry in the process. Om has infinite power and patience to protect you, love you and accept you as you are.

I have tried to demystify the practice by describing it in simple language understandable to modern readers. In this book, I have offered safe and simple know-how and practices that would help anyone willing, to begin the practice right away. There are insights and techniques in the meditation section that, I believe, will be of help to the advanced practitioners too. These practices will help to provide deep relaxation, stress-relief, a greater Self-awareness, a sustained sense of well-being and even a glimpse of the supreme reality that exists beyond the domain of the physical senses and the mind.

PART I

OM CHANTING

What is Om?

Everyone wants to be blissful and happy. This desire lies at the very core of our inner being because our true nature is ever-blissful. Chanting and meditation of Om is the way to reach and abide in that ever-blissful nature underlying our surface personality. This is bliss for no reason at all. It is unconditional bliss, a bliss that is everlasting, un-decaying, pure and stainless. Om is our blissful Self.

Contrary to the popular notion, Om is neither a symbol, nor a sound; nor is it an entity sitting high above the cloud somewhere in this universe. Then what it is really? Om is our all pervading higher Self. It is the soundless sound of existence, which the Zen Buddhists refer as 'the sound of one hand clapping'. No human vocal cord can imitate this soundless sound accurately. Neither is it a symbol. The symbol, the sound, these are used as a finger pointing to the moon. The finger is not the moon; however, it helps one to find the moon. This is so with the use of the symbol and the chanting of the Om. They help you to connect with your higher Self. The sound of Om awakens our slumbering soul to recognize its divinity.

Om is the mysterious cosmic energy that is the substratum of all the things and all the beings of the entire universe. It is an eternal song of the Divine. It is continuously resounding in silence on the background of everything that exists. Our ordinary human ear can not hear it. Through Om chanting we try to attune with this universal energy that brings all auspiciousness in our lives.

Om is the Brahman (the infinite cosmic consciousness), the indestructible Life force. Om is this universe. It is the nameless, the Divine. It is the totality of you, I, and the whole creation. It is the totality of past, present and future of this existence. At the same time, it is the eternal now, unfolding this very moment. It is life-eternal flowing through this temporal existence.

Normally, we identify ourselves with the outermost layer of our personality, which is always in a state of turmoil with numerous thoughts, feelings, emotions, judgments, patterns, knowledge and imaginations. However, beneath these layers, there exists our true nature, which is unborn, undying, un-decaying and full of peace, love and bliss. Om chanting and meditation is all about getting connected with our true nature.

Om chanting helps us to transcend continuous identification with our outermost layer. It helps us to reconnect to our immortal nature. It allows every cell of our being to vibrate with the rhythm of the unconditional divine love and peacc. Om chanting is an effective but very gentle way of training the mind to develop inner strength and freedom from turmoil, leading on to clarity and understanding.

Om means happiness. Om means peace. Om means infinite bliss. Om means support-less, limitless, unconditional, pure love. Om means abundance. Om means fulfillment. Om means flow of life. Om means all auspiciousness. Om means everything, the Whole. Om means all positive things of life.

The Chanting

Try it for yourself and see the difference it makes. Om chanting destroys inner conflicts, negative beliefs and destructive conditioning of a person. As Om is the fountain of life, light, warmth, love and well-being, the soft intonation of Om transforms all negative thoughts, beliefs and anxieties in to positive and life-giving vibrations. Om chanting burns away the Karmic seeds. Om chanting has several spiritual, psychological and health benefits.

Do it daily, as little as you can. Om chanting is a systematic gentle way to make your mind quiet so that you can connect to your true Self, which is the source of everlasting joy, bliss and peace. There are four methods or techniques of Om chanting; Loud Om chanting, Mental soft chanting, Listening and witnessing and Merging.

For starting the practice of Om chanting, you do not have to believe in something. You do not need to spend a single penny for that. You do not need to join any organization. You do not need to learn any complicated philosophy or techniques. Om chanting is already happening in your blood, in your heart, in your brain. It is happening in your every cell, every moment. You only need to tune with it, turn your attention inward, listen to that and merge with that. Om is the mantra of integration. Om chanting is the art of flowing with the whole.

Om chanting is an ancient, nonreligious, non-sectarian technique. It has absolutely nothing to do with any organizational affiliation. The Om chanting cures a being at all levels, physical, emotional, mental and spiritual. It has healing effects to clear away blockages. It purifies the body, mind and enlivens the spirit. Do it in a relaxed manner, at a pace, time and duration that is comfortable for you, fitting with your lifestyle. Your inner Guru is always there to guide you. Rely and trust on that.

Om: The Mysterious Word of Words

Om contains within it all that is sacred and mundane. It is the mysterious expression of the infinity, timelessness, eternity, wisdom, non-locality and non-duality. It is our true nature, our higher self, the core of our inner being. It was the first cosmic sound for manifestation that emerged from the Unmanifest. It is the Word, the holy monosyllable. It is the nectar of immortality, the light of all lights, and the life of all lives.

It is an eternal melody of love, peace and harmony. It is the sacred song of the Divine. Om means fearlessness. Om means protection. Om means acceptance. It accepts you as you are at this very moment.

The whole Mandukya Upanishad is dedicated to describe the meaning and glory of Om, which is also uttered as AUM. Among the three letters, the letter A represents the beginning, the letter U represents the growth and the letter M represents dissolution. Therefore, the letters A, U and M stand for creation, preservation and dissolution.

This one syllable represents the entire cosmos. It is the common denominator of everything. Om is the creator, the process of creation and the creation. The true meaning of Om can not be really expressed in words. Om is the mantra for feeling of oneness with the whole of existence. Known as the most secret and sacred word of the existence. It is the primordial sound, the source of the whole creation. Om has a magic about it, a virtue, which directly brings all your thoughts and feelings in to a state of harmony. It brings the mind in a state where the ego of the seeker is merged into the existence, where there is no difference between the knower, known and the knowing. In such a state, the true meaning of Om is revealed.

What is Om Symbol?

The symbol of Om mantra is ॐ. It is a symbol of love, purity, happiness, peacefulness and abundance. If you meditate on different parts of the lighted symbol of Om, different aspect of the existence will be revealed gradually to you and finally you will be merged into its essence. It is believed, that if you pay respect to the symbol, you are paying respect to your inner Self, which will bring all good to you.

Color of Om Symbol

Technically, there is no restriction about the color of the symbol. Om is the symbol of auspiciousness. One should meditate on Om with a color that creates well being and auspicious vibration on mind. Normally, bright white color is considered as the color of Om symbol. The seven colors of white represent the seven aspects of the Om symbol. The color of Sun as observed from the earth is the color of Om. As we know, the color of Sun varies throughout the day from red, orange or yellow to silvery white, milky white and golden red; similarly the color of Om also varies depending on our choice, mood or personality. However, golden and red colored Om symbols are most common. Visualizing bright golden colored Om during meditation is a common practice.

Sound of Om

Om is known as "*Udgita*", which means the song that spontaneously arises from the soul. The sound of Om is the sound of the Self. The sound of "Om" is known as "*Anahata*", which means un-struck sound. All other ordinary sounds in the universe emerge out of one object striking another or out of frictional force. The sound of Om is un-struck sound, which can not be generated by something or by some means. It is a self-producing sound. It existed before the universe was born. The mystical sound of Om is continuously happening in the background of everything. Our ordinary sense perceptions normally can not recognize that un-struck sound of Om. But as we tune our internal faculties by Om chanting and Om meditations, or by any other means, we can feel the beauty and splendor of the un-struck sound. Om is a living phenomenon. The consciousness of Om is higher than our normal waking consciousness. Om is our higher Self. As we look forward to it and embraces it in our inner world, the mystery of the Om is revealed to us.

Om is known as the mother of everything, the source of all. This Universe is the child of Om. The sound of Om is often referred as Primordial sound. It is the sound that manifested itself during the birth of the Universe.

However, at the outer and physical level, the sound of bell, the sound from conch shell and the sound of ocean waves are considered as the sound of Om.

Om and the Higher Dimensions

Upanishad declared "Beyond the body and senses is the mind; beyond the mind is the intellect; higher than the intellect is the great Self; higher than the Self is the unmanifest. Beyond the unmanifest is the Supreme Reality, the all pervading and imperceptible. Having realized that, the embodied self becomes liberated and attains Immortality." – [Katha Upanishad 1:3:10-11].

There is a higher dimension beyond this time and space and that higher dimension can be realized by this very body and mind, if we are tuned to that by Om meditation and Om chanting. With the penetrating wisdom of meditation we can realize the things beyond the space-time trajectory. We can realize the unified field of cosmic awareness.

According to the contemporary theory of physics our Universe was born roughly 13.7 billion years ago. Normally, general theory of relativity and quantum mechanics are very successful in explaining the mystery of the universe. However, both general theory of relativity and quantum mechanics break down in explaining the first moment of Big Bang. When the physicists attempted to extrapolate the general theory of relativity at time equal to zero or when time is negative, they reach the point where temperature, density and gravity in the model become infinite. At this infinitely strong gravity, the space and time collapsed. This point of zero volume and infinite density at time zero is known as singularity. At this point, the mystic concept of infinity of Om, which existed before the creation of the time and space, sounds valid; because what existed before the creation of time and space is beyond the boundaries of the contemporary modern physics. It is also beyond our normal sensory perceptions. The existence of higher dimensions is now widely accepted by the physicists. Om the Divine song is at the same time Symmetry, Supersymmetry, broken Symmetry, and the unbroken Symmetry of Nature.

How to Chant Om?

Om chanting is a journey from the gross to subtle, and ultimately to the subtlest aspect of reality. It is a journey from a noisy mind to a still mind. It is movement from doing to non-doing. It is a movement towards stillness. It is an art of turning your gaze inward.

Om chanting is a systematic gentle way to make your mind quiet so that you can connect to your true Self, which is the source of everlasting joy, bliss and peace. Loving the Om means loving yourself, your own Self.

Om chanting is a creative art, not just mechanical repetition of a word. Om is known as Pranava, which means new, the ever fresh. So, each uttering of Om mantra is always new, unique and fresh. It is unique not only because of the variations of the sound but also due to the variation in the degree of love and devotion that we put in to the chanting. We all are unique in our temperament and nature. Therefore, our utterances of Om should be spontaneous and unique.

Don't worry about the perfection of your chanting. Since Om is the Cosmic sound, the eternal seed-vibration of the universe, no human vocal cord can produce it perfectly.

Chant the Om sound in your own way, in a relaxed manner. The feeling of relaxation is the most important factor when you are chanting. Om chanting should be almost effortless. The more you put effort on chanting, the more you are away from the goal.

Initially, efforts are required just to remove the thoughts, the past patterns. Gradually, as you master the art, Om chanting will be an effortless phenomenon. Allow the Om to unfold in its own way, in your consciousness.

Set yourself a time for how long you want to chant, and stick to it. Remember, it does not really matter whether you chant for five, ten or thirty minutes. The point is to set a time and stick to the daily practice of it. Just be determined to keep chanting until the time is up.

Sit comfortably, keep your back straight and hold your hands together. Keep your eyes closed. Mentally repeat the word "O-o-o-M-m-m," slowly and rhythmically with your out-breath. Do not disturb your normal breathing pattern. You need not chant "Om" in every out-breath. You may give a gap for one or two breaths and then again, you can start chanting slowly. The length of your chant should exactly match the normal length of your out-breath. If your, out-breath is short, chant short "Om". If your out-breath is long, chant long "Om". Think, as if, the out-breath itself is chanting "Om".

After your practice matures, you can feel as if each cell of your body is chanting Om. In reality, the vibration of the cells in your body itself signifies the vibration of the holy Om. It is the spontaneous chanting that is happening in your body. You just need to be aware of it and feel it, while you are chanting. Your chanting should be accompanied with feeling to provide best result. While chanting, you may feel your whole body from the tip of your toe to the top of your head. Feel as if peace, happiness and blissfulness of Om envelopes you and gradually merge yourself into that blissfulness. Soft chanting of Om will quickly move you beyond your constant mental chatter into the clarity of awareness itself. Then, finally stop the chanting and just witness the sensation in your body. Just witness the feelings in silence.

In Om chanting, basically, you are calling your own Self, your own divine nature, your most loveable inner essence, which is full of love, happiness and joy. So, techniques may be important for the initial stages, but finally, it is love for your Self, which matters.

When to Chant Om?

When you get up naturally in the morning, when the environment is peaceful and joyful, is the best time for Om chanting. Early morning Om chanting will put your life into the rhythm with the life of the universe.

Otherwise, there is no specific time for Om chanting. Depending on your life style, when you are relaxed, when you are not hurried, you can choose a time of 10 minutes daily for soft Om chanting. Normally, during the time of Sunrise or Sunset and even before doing deep meditation, doing 5 minutes of Om chanting will make your mind relaxed and focused. Before going to bed and after you wake up from the bed, you can do soft or mental Om chanting for a few minutes.

Do not do Om chanting immediately after the meal because as the energy will rise to your brain, it will slow down your digestive process.

Om chanting is helpful when you want to remove unwanted thoughts and vibrations. If you chant Om mentally, very slowly in a relaxed manner with your out-breath, it will make the environment peaceful and happy.

Where to Chant Om?

Select a place where you will not be disturbed, wherever you can sit comfortably and peacefully for as little as five minutes without distractions. When you get up naturally in the morning, you can chant Om, sitting on your bed. If you can have a separate room for meditation on Om, that will be good. However, you may even set a corner of your bedroom for that purpose. You can chant Om for as little as two minutes sitting in your car at the parking space.

On holidays if you happen to visit a quiet scenic place, that would be an ideal place for remembering Om. Om chanting puts your life into the rhythm with the life-flow of the universe. Hence, there is no specific time or place for Om chanting. Depending on your life style, when you are relaxed, when you are not hurried, any quiet place is good for chanting Om.

Why to chant Om?

The mysterious energy of Om is reverberating in silence as the substratum of the universe. It is the life of our lives. Our ordinary life is a sacred expression of Om. It exists as deep inner peace at the core of our being. Om chanting gradually leads us towards a silent awakening in that inner peace, which already exists within us. Living in deep inner peace is a silent revolution that can eventually change the destiny of the entire human race. A single sunflower contains the seeds for thousands of new plants. When one person becomes peaceful, his or her inner peace is radiated to make others peaceful. This inner peace spreads out into the environment and ultimately to the entire universe.

Soft vocal chanting or silent intonation of Om creates a state of restful alertness that powerfully draws the awareness deep within to provide a deep sense of calm. Om chanting increases the clarity and focus of mind, improves concentration and sharpens the memory. Om chanting decreases the restless tendency of mind to generate peace and happiness within.

Om chanting destroys inner conflicts, negative beliefs and destructive conditioning of a person. As Om is the fountain of life, light, warmth, love and well-being, the soft intonation of Om transforms all negative thoughts, beliefs and anxieties in to positive and life-giving vibrations. Om chanting burns away the Karmic seeds, which produces negative thoughts.

Om chanting integrates the personality at all levels of being, thus generating a sense of light, love and total well-being. Om chanting is helpful when you want to remove unwanted thoughts and vibrations. If you chant Om mentally, very slowly in a relaxed manner with your out-breath, it will make you and your environment peaceful and happy.

So, Om chanting is not just for your personal benefits, though there are so many of them. By chanting a single Om you are getting connected to the whole cosmos at a deep inner level of your being. When are being peaceful and relaxed through the Om chanting, your environment too is positively affected.

How to Pronounce Om?

Om is known as "Ek aksharam Brahman", which means Om is a single letter mantra, symbolizing the supreme reality of the infinite existence. It is a process of increasing your awareness about the subtlest vibrations in your body and finally merging with your inner being. Om sound is considered as the combination of three letters A, U, M and Silence.

In Sanskrit, when 'A' and 'U' are combined they produce the sound of 'O'. During vocal Om chanting, it is pronounced as "O-O-O-M-M-M...". While chanting, the mantra should produce some inner resonance in your body. When the mantra is chanted with devotion, these vibrations of the letter M tune up the energy points and produces calming effect on your body and mind. When uttering 'O' part of the Om, mouth will remain open, while uttering the 'M' part, mouth will remain closed.

While chanting, keep in mind that a complete Om sound has four parts, that is, "O" + "M" + Humming sound of "M", which is known as *"ardha-matra"* + Silence. If you are new to Om chanting, it will be better if the "O" part is longer than the others.

However, for inner Om chanting, the Om is considered as a single letter. It is pronounced exactly as 'om' is pronounced in 'h**om**e' or 'R**om**e'. Since Om is the Cosmic sound, the eternal seed-vibration of the universe, no human vocal cord can produce it perfectly. So, success of Om chanting does not depend much on how to pronounce. It absolutely depends on your feeling of love, devotion and your willingness to move in to the deeper silence and peace of your inner being.

Om and the Energy Centers

Chakras are the astral energy centers in our body. By focusing our attention to specific area in the body we can direct the vital energy to move into that area. There are nine major chakras and twenty one minor chakras in the body. Balancing these thirty chakras is vital for our overall happiness. Our physical and mental well-beings are directly related to the quality of energy that passes through these energy centers. During soft Om chanting, the energy of the Om produces a feeling of wellbeing in the body. As we meditate or chant Om on these energy centers the positive energy of the Om balances the energy centers and produces a soothing and calming effect. We can balance the energy at any location just by visualizing that we are doing mental Om chanting in that location.

There are nine major energy centers in the body. Five of them are located along the spine, two in the head and two near the navel. Among these centers, two energy centers important. The energy center located in the ' the eye brow and the energy center, which is located just one inch above the navel point. These are the places of Om meditation for the beginners. During meditation, one can visualize a bright golden sun of Om in these locations. Navel is known as the fire center of the body. Too much concentration, awareness or focus in this area may produce heat. Hence, too much concentration in this area must be avoided. This place should be used just for igniting the vital energy. As meditation progresses, the awareness should move from this point to the middle of the eye brow and to the top of the skull through the spinal cord.

Om chanting opens the "Dasham Duar" the mystical tenth spiritual gateway located at the top of the skull. The un-struck blissful sound of Om is heard at this tenth gate. It is not a physical door. It is a psychic door. Normally, it remains closed by attachment and aversions. In the state of purified consciousness, the gate opens up and a nectar-like essence is dripped from this point to fulfill the entire body and mind with highest relaxation and blissfulness, and realization of supreme consciousness happens.

Om and Expression of Divinity

We are divine cosmic flowers. Great wisdom, deep calmness, peace, happiness, blissfulness, sharing, caring, compassion and celebrations are the hallmarks of divinity. Our mind and body always want to manifest the divine expression. The body and mind are continuously looking for their eternal connections with the divinity, because divinity is our true nature. However, the expression of Divinity is a progressive, slow and subtle process. It takes certain time to bloom in its fullest form.

There are seven main phases of the expression of divine energy during Om chanting and meditation. These seven phases are: the dormant phase, the phase of transformation, the flowering phase, the phase of fragrance radiation, the phase of attraction of cosmic consciousness and finally, the phase of unification with cosmic Om consciousness. Each of these phases has additional stages of development.

Normally, the human divinity remains dormant in its potential form, with occasional flowering. Negative thoughts and unhealthy tendencies like jealousy, hatred, anger and fear work as divinity-barrier and do not allow the psychic petals to open. These cause the psychic energy to flow downwards. However, with proper nourishing and caring with Om mantra, the wonderful blossom unfolds progressively, one petal after another, till the thousand-petal lotus blossoms. When the rays of the cosmic consciousness touch the petals we feel the elixir of enlightenment.

Om chanting and meditation is the process of crossing the divinity-barrier. When potent divinity within us is ignited with silent Om mantra, the divinity-barrier can be crossed easily. The quality and techniques of Om chanting and Om meditation varies according to the phases of expression of the divinity. It requires fine tuning as we progress forward.

Om Chanting Methods

Om chanting is the process of synchronization of body, mind, breath, intellect, spirit and the cosmos. Rhythm, relaxation, generation of subtle vibration in the whole body and feeling of that vibration are the key components of Om chanting technique. Scripture suggests many techniques for chanting the Om, depending on the personality and mental state of the person. However, it can be classified into two broad groups; soft chanting and loud chanting.

Depending on the state of our consciousness, there are four different types of Om chanting practices. They are Vocal Om chanting, Mental Om chanting, Witnessing of Om and Transcendental awareness of Om.

At the beginning, vocal Om chanting is generally prescribed for about three weeks. After that, you may reduce the period of your vocal Om chanting and introduce mental Om chanting. Continue this combination of first vocal Om chanting for a few minutes and then mental Om chanting, for about two months.

A combination of ten minutes of vocal Om chanting, five minutes of mental Om chanting, five minutes of listening to the inner Om, that is, witnessing the feelings, and 10 minutes of silence can be practiced at a later stage.

Again, depending on the duration of each Om, Om chanting is classified as long, short and medium chanting. Broadly speaking, if one Om chanting takes more than ten seconds it is considered as long Om chanting. If it is less than three seconds, it is considered as a short Om. In between three to ten seconds, it is considered as medium Om chanting.

A combination of twenty long Om chanting, forty medium Om chanting and forty short Om chanting in three cycles followed by long silence is also practiced. For this type of Om chanting the help of a competent teacher is advisable.

At the beginning, you may practice long and vocal Om chanting followed by silence. This long and vocal Om chanting is quite common. It is a kind of natural

Pranayam. You may practice it in empty stomach in the morning.

As we have mentioned earlier, the Om sound is made of the combination of the letters A, U, M and the silence. When 'A' and 'U' are uttered together it makes the sound 'O'. At the initial stage, you should give more emphasis on the letter 'O'. As you progress you put your awareness on the 'M' aspect of Om, and finally on the silence.

At the initial stages of your Om chanting, during the chanting, you must keep your awareness within your body, preferably below your heart center. As you progress, you may rotate your awareness from head to toe and from toe to head. Finally, as you master the art of Om chanting you will be automatically able to put your awareness either at the middle of your eyebrow or at the top of your skull. Do not jump to the eyebrow or to the top of your skull from the beginning. We have discussed below more about humming Om chanting methods.

Gamma Waves and Humming Om

Om chanting is often practiced as humming like the bees. The humming type of Om chanting is the most common and most useful. In this type of Om chanting, lips will remain closed and the long Om sound is to be pronounced gently and smoothly through the nose area. More emphasis is to be given on the "...mmmmm" part of the vibration. The feeling of the resonance of the Om vibration in the body is vital. Humming Om chanting should be done in a very low and relaxed voice with a positive state of mind.

There are several pathways in the body in which the vibration of Om flows during the chanting. However, the ‘Prefrontal pathway' and the ‘Hara pathway’ for humming Om chanting are most important. Recently, scientists like Jon Lundberg reported that humming near the sinuses releases 15-fold higher level of nitric-oxide (NO). According to the recent scientific research, nitric-oxide is one of the most vital components which improve the immune system, the nervous system and the cardiovascular system. In fact, the 1998 Nobel Prize was awarded for the discovery of nitric-oxide as a weapon against infection and high blood pressure.

Three parameters are very important for humming Om chanting. They are the point of awareness, the pathway of the Om vibration and the duration of the Om chanting in each point. Normally, the ‘Hara pathway’ is the most significant one. The ‘Hara’ area lies just 1.5 inch below the navel, which is often used as the starting and ending area of Om chanting, while other areas are covered in between. For example, in a typical 5-3-7-3-3, humming Om chanting, five times humming is done in the Hara area, then three times in the heart area, then seven times in the eye-brow area, then three times in the heart area and then again three times in the Hara area. Total duration may vary, but the relative ratio of the awareness in different areas should be maintained. It is a very slow process. Relax for a few seconds and note the sensations before moving the awareness from one center to another. For safety purpose, the movement of awareness should be always directed along the spinal column only. Advanced meditators often use specific pathways for specific purposes. Often these pathways pass through different glands inside the body.

There are other pathways in the hands, upper palate, throat, brain and other areas of the body. Whole body Om chanting and criss-cross Om chanting are also very effective. In criss-cross Om chanting, alternatively two paths are followed. The first path is: right hand palm, right-shoulder, brain, left-shoulder, left-hand palm and then again back to the right hand palm. The second path is up and down along the spinal cord and the brain. Awareness of humming Om chanting is rotated alternatively along these two paths. These pathways are not rigid, rely on the wisdom of Om while practicing it.

Sambhabi mudra and bhramari pranayama are the two associated yoga techniques which are closely related to humming types of Om chanting. Recent scientific and clinical studies observed that bhramari pranayama produces Gamma waves in the brain. Gamma waves are considered as the critical component for brain synchronization, temporal binding of the brain activities and higher order cognitive processing. Humming Om chanting has direct correlation with the Gamma wave generation. Regular and systematic humming Om chanting has a lot of healing effects and it prepares the body and mind for realizing the limitless nature of the Self.

Bhramari Om Chanting

The Sanskrit word "Bhramari" means the humming sound of the bees. Bhramari Om chanting is done in sitting posture, with spine erect and relaxed. During this type of Om chanting mouth and the lips will remain closed.

Sit in cross-legged position or on a chair with spine erect and legs placed squarely on the ground. Then place your palms on the both sides of the head and close the eyes. Use the thumbs to keep the ears closed. Place your index fingers on both side of your temple, the middle fingers loosely on the closed eye lids, the ring fingers below the nostrils and the little fingers below the lips. In a relaxed state just observe your breath for three time. Now, while exhaling, in a relaxed manner chant long "Ommmmm", though nostril with your lips remaining closed. This will create a humming sound which could be heard by a person sitting near you. Feel the resonance and vibrations of the sound Om in the sinuses and the head.

Remember that both the inhalation and exhalation should be through the nostrils and mouth should be closed. This simple practice of Bhramari Om chanting is very helpful in making the breath smooth and adding clarity to the mind by quieting the mind. The gamma wave emitted by this process synchronizes the brain by making it prepared for cognitive processing of a higher order.

Five Basic Principles of Om Chanting

There are five basic principles of Om chanting. They can be summarized as follows:

The first aspect is restful deep relaxation and alertness. During Om chanting, your relaxed alertness should be such that you will know the subtle changes in the bodily sensations, feelings and the rhythm of breathing.

The second aspect of Om chanting is the slow but long humming of the word Om. Om chanting is most effective, where mouth and lips remains closed, breathing is done slowly through the nasal passages, and awareness rotates in different paths.

The third aspect of Om chanting is to keep your focus on the length of each Om chanting and synchronize it with the normal length of your exhalation. Chanting should be done only during exhalation. Before the start of the Om chanting, you must observe your normal duration for inhalation and exhalation. During Om chanting your exhalation period should be slightly longer. You need to slowly use different portions of the word OM and the silence to elongate the exhalation period in a very comfortable and relaxed manner.

The fourth important aspect is moving the focus of attention along the central nervous system, specially, along the middle of the spinal cord. Initially, you can keep your attention on your lower abdomen for a few moments. This is the point about 1.5 inches below the navel point. But finally, during Om chanting, the awareness should travel to and fro along the middle of the spinal cord. Normally, our sensory information flows in an automatic bottom up way and back to the front of the brain. At the beginning of the Om chanting, for a few minutes the awareness should move from the front to the back of the brain and then top to down along the spinal cord. After that the attention should be allowed to flow freely along the middle of the spinal cord.

The fifth aspect of Om chanting will purely focus on the sound of Om, thereby cutting, nullifying or eliminating all other thoughts. Thus a restful silence will ensue, creating a very relaxed state of mind.

These five aspects should be practiced separately in different sessions, in the beginning. Finally, when you master them all, you can synchronize and practice them in a single sitting. As you progress, your awareness will be settled automatically either at the middle of your eyebrow or at the top of your skull for a long duration.

In a state of perfection with your Om chanting, you will be automatically maintaining an optimum level of oxygen and carbon dioxide balance in your body. Normally, with proper Om chanting, the oxygen utilization rate per breath increases substantially. Hence, as you progress in Om chanting, your normal breathing rate per minute will go down and your health and overall well being will improve significantly.

You should be your own judge, in this practice. At any moment if you feel discomfort or uneasiness, you must be sure that you are going out of the track. If that happens, stop the practice for a few days, understand the basics of the process and adjust it in a different way, which seems more suitable for you.

The Mental or Soft Om Chanting

In soft chanting, you are calling your beloved. Call your inner beloved in your own style, in a style that gives you maximum satisfaction, peace and happiness. You are your own judge. You are calling your most dearest and nearest one, who is always protective and kind to you. So chant very silently and softly 'Om', ‘Om’, 'Om'.

Thc mental Om chanting leads to transcendental awareness. After you practice the mental chanting for certain duration, just remember the "Om" and feel your oneness with it. A time will come when you will merge with it, with the innermost bliss of the Self. By chanting Om, you will be connected with the whole, which is the source of infinite happiness.

In meditation penetrate deep into the word "Om". Gradually the word will disappear and only the silence will remain. The word is just a support, the meaning is within you. Om brings out that meaning which is hidden in your soul. Om is a living phenomena and every living thing has its mood. Depending on its mood the wisdom will be revealed to you.

Om Chanting and our Personality

As individuals, we are all unique in our personalities. Nevertheless, we are all manifestations of the Om. Om is like a great ocean of which individuals are like waves. A wave can not exist, independent of the ocean. Similarly, an ocean can not be defined without its waves. A wave has no boundary to define it, though it maintains its individual shape. Similarly we are boundless and one with the great ocean of Om, though we maintain our unique personalities as individuals.

The mystery of Om chanting is its ability to go deeper and deeper into our inner silence. There are four levels of our personality. First is the outer physical level, where there is a specific form. All our activities and speech happen in this level. Then there is the mental level, where thoughts and emotions take place. Then there is the subtler vibration of the causal level that defines our individuality; and, on the fourth level of our being, we are all one with the transcendental reality that exists beyond the states of waking, dreaming and deep sleep. This is the center of supreme peace that exists at the core of our being.

All these layers of our persona are manifestations of Om at different levels. The outer physical level is called the 'Vaikhari' or manifestation at the grossest level. The word Vaikhari, in Sanskrit, means flowering. So, our physical persona is the 'Vaikhari Om'.

Then there is the mental level, which is called the 'Madhyama'. Madhyama, in Sanskrit, means that which is in the middle; it is that which is in between the seed and the flower. It is like the tree, which bears the flowers. It is our thoughts that bear the flowers of our speech and actions. So, the mental level of our persona is the 'Madhyama Om'.

On the third level of our personality, there is the notion of individuality that is the seed of all our thoughts, speeches and actions. It is called the 'Pashyanti'. 'Pashyanti', in Sanskrit, means that, which witnesses. Our sense of individuality, as the 'I am', witnesses all our thoughts, speech and actions. This level of witnessing is 'Pashyanti Om'.

Beyond these three levels of our personality lies the fourth. This is our transcendental, unborn nature. It is beyond thought, the supreme, un-decaying, unmodified state; a place that is unfathomable. It is the level of Supreme peace, where we are one with all that exists. This is defined as the 'Para'. 'Para', in Sanskrit, means, that which transcends. It is that level of our existence, which transcends birth and death and all worldly dualities. This level is 'Para Om', the supreme Silence from which all manifestations emerge and in to which all manifestations are dissolved. It is the abode of all auspiciousness.

Om and Personality Integration

The four methods of Om chanting, discussed earlier, affects these four levels of our personality. In order to be able to align ourselves with the universal energy, we need to integrate all the layers of our personality. This is done by four types of Om chanting.

Vocal Om chanting affects the outermost or physical layer of your personality. To affect this layer you need to chant the Om mantra loudly and long. Do it like "OoooMmmm…","OoooMmmm…", OoooMmmm…". At this level, efforts are required. It relaxes your body and has a soothing effect on the mind.

To affect the mental layer of your personality, soft mental chanting of the Om should be undertaken along with the loud vocal chanting. Your lips will remain close. You may chant along with your breath. This should be done with minimum effort. Thus, you are gradually moving towards the source. Outer layers will merge and be one with the inner mental layer. Your mind will become more silent. You will start feeling peace throughout your body, at this stage.

Next, to affect and integrate the causal and the third layer of your personality, stop the mental chanting and silently witness the resonance or vibration of Om within the cells of your body.

In the first level your lips, that are parts of the physical body, were active; in the second level, your lips remains closed and the mind is active in uttering Om; now, in the third stage you shut down both your lips and your mind, to move deeper in to the witnessing level of your being. You may also witness the sound of your breath as the effortless happening of Om in your body. To reach the fourth level of your being, even the witnessing needs to be dropped. You become very still, to be one with the blissful silence of your inner being.

If you practice this way, all the layers of your personality will be integrated to manifest as calm, poise, joy and enthusiasm in your life. An integrated personality is a gift of the Divine that remains centered and happy and works for the benefit of all. The practice of Om chanting enables you to attain this seemingly impossible feat in this modern era of speed, haste and distraction.

The 'Para level' of your being is beyond manifestation. It is when everything is merged in to supreme stillness. It is a state of infinite peace. It is reached when your mind is totally dissolved. Initially, it may be there only for a split of moment. As you practice more and more you will get the taste of it.

We are nothing but unique expressions of the supreme silence. Out of silence, we manifested, and into the silence, we melt again. This state is variously described as the silence, the void, the emptiness, which is a state of absolute peace, harmony and pure love; it is our innermost core. Om chanting is a process of moving from outer noise and chattering to the innermost core of deep silence.

Do's and Don'ts of Om Chanting

There are certain points that need to be remembered before you undertake the Om chanting.

Do's of Om Chanting

1. During Om chanting, always sit in a comfortable straight and upright position.
2. Make Om chanting as a part of your daily practice.
3. Always keep the body and mind relaxed as much as possible and chant in a rhythmic way and in harmonious tone.
4. Drink sufficient water 15 minutes before and after Om chanting.

5. At the end of the Om chanting and meditation, sit or lie down silently for a few minutes.
6. This practice spreads the energy evenly all over the body.
7. There are several techniques for Om chanting. Do a little bit of experiments with these techniques to see which suits you best.
8. Though, people generally benefit from Om chanting, test it for yourself to find how it works for you.
9. Do some light free hand exercises everyday to spread the energy evenly throughout the body.

Don'ts of Om Chanting

1. Do not practice Om chanting just after a meal.
2. Do not chant Om very fast and in an erratic manner.
3. Avoid mechanical and unaware Om chanting.
4. Never do Om chanting for a long duration, if you are a beginner.
5. Do not practice Om chanting when you are depressed.
6. Do not practice loud Om chanting if you have digestive problems.
7. Any time if you feel any discomfort stop the practice for several days and gradually come back to the practice, when you are comfortable again.

Benefits of Om Chanting

Om chanting sets up a harmonic vibration in the environment and in our whole nervous system. This harmonic vibration generates peace, joy and happiness in our inner as well as outer environment. By Om chanting the cells of our body get revitalized. Particularly, the humming kind of Om chanting produces a gentle massage in the brain cells, which produces happiness and fulfillment in our lives. If you are happy, you radiate your happiness in the environment. As the energy of happiness grows in the environment, it positively affects all the beings in the entire universe. That is the greatest contribution, the most precious gift we can offer to the universe. We are inseparable part of the universe. We are indivisible part of a great energy ocean that permeates, surrounds and engulfs all the beings in the entire universe. So, if we are happy, if we are at peace, the universe is happy, the universe will be at peace.

Spiritual Benefits:

Om makes us feel at one with the cosmos. A great attunement happens through the vibration of Om, when chanted in a harmonious and relaxed manner. Om chanting makes you fearless and blissful. As you feel oneness with the universe, greater love, compassion, peace and harmony manifests in your life. You radiate your peace and happiness in the environment.

Deep silence and calm resides within our inner being behind the chatter and turmoil of mental activities. Om chanting allows us to reconnect with that deep silence of our being.

Enlightenment is being one with the Whole. It is being at a state of permanent happiness, joy, fulfillment and profound inner peace that is unruffled by any external phenomena. Om leads you to that.

Health Benefits:

Om chanting promotes deep breathing with prolonged exhalations, thereby activating the parasympathetic nervous system that produces relaxation response in the body and mind.

Om chanting increases the flow of oxygen in blood, thus promoting health, vigor, healing and immunity.

Om chanting tones up the nervous system and clears away subtle blockages to revitalize the body. It releases the tensions and stress, and relaxes the muscles and nerves. It is like smearing all the ramifications of the nerves with honey. The effect is soothing and relaxing.

Mental chanting of Om provides rests to the vital organs of the body and balances subtle energies of the body thereby accelerating healing.

Moreover, Om chanting brings the "limbic system" or the “emotional brain” under control. Om meditation activates the frontal lobe of the brain and releases the unnecessary emotions generated by the limbic regions of the brain. Specially, Om chanting controls the amygdala and the hypothalamic-pituitary-adrenal (HPA) axis, the stress producing unit of the brain. Om meditation optimizes the central coordination system in the brain. It improves the interaction among the brain’s limbic system, which controls emotions and the prefrontal brain responsible for higher cognition.

Psychological Benefits:

Loud chanting or silent intonation of Om creates a state of restful alertness that powerfully draws the awareness deep within, to provide a deep sense of calm. Om chanting increases the clarity and focus of mind, improves concentration and sharpens the memory.

Om chanting decreases the restless tendency of mind to generate peace and happiness within. Om chanting helps us to attune with the inner silence and peace. The silence revitalizes the body and purifies the mind.

Om chanting destroys inner conflicts, negative beliefs and destructive conditioning. As Om is the very embodiment of life, light, warmth, love and well-being, the soft intonation of Om transforms all negative thoughts, beliefs and anxieties in to positive and life-giving vibrations.

Om chanting integrates the personality at all levels of being, thus generating a sense of light, love and total well-being.

Om: Brainwaves & Consciousness

Our brain functions at various speeds depending on the levels of our consciousness. Om chanting is deeply associated with the speed of our brain functions and the various levels of our consciousness. The sound Om is constituted of three syllables; A, U and M represents the three different states of our consciousness. The table below gives various interpretation of the letters A,U,M and the silence. When we do aware Om chanting or Om meditation, several regions of the prefrontal cortex operates at 40 Hz frequency. However, major regions of the brain, moves from normal beta level to deeper and deeper levels.

Table 1: Om (AUM), the State of Consciousness & Brainwaves of the Major Brain Regions.

Om Sound	Level of Consciousness	Brain Wave State	Brain Wave Frequency	State of Consciousness
A	Waking	Beta	13-30 Hz	Highly Active
U	Dreaming	Alpha	8-13 Hz	Light Meditation
M	Deep Sleep	Theta	4-8 Hz	Deep Meditation
Silence	Restful Deep Awareness	Delta + Gamma	1-4 Hz & 30-50 Hz	Samadhi

At the beta stage of functioning the brain operates at a highly active level, continuously receiving, interpreting, analyzing and judging the data and inputs from external sources and internal source of memory reserve. It is when we operate in our normal waking hours.

At the alpha stage, the brain operates at a quieter, relaxed level, with the judgment and analyzing faculty of mind almost at rest. It happens when you dream, listen to some soothing music or relax in a meditative mood. It is from this level that any original idea and works of art and creativity flow out to manifest. Most of the significant scientific discoveries have happened when the scientists have entered this level knowingly or unknowingly.

At the theta stage, the functioning of the brain is reduced to a minimum. It is when the judging, analyzing and interpreting faculty of mind is completely at rest. It is a state of deep relaxation. This stage is highly rejuvenating for the body and mind. Healing also happens at this level. It is when you enter the deep sleep or a deep level of meditative absorption. We all know how a sound dreamless sleep refreshes and rejuvenate the body and mind. At this stage, you know nothing, interpret nothing and possess nothing. Still this state is so much peace giving. The modern science also recognizes the healing power of deep sleep.

But apart from the state of deep sleep state where you know nothing, there is another state unknown to most people which resembles deep sleep except for the fact that you remain completely awake at a state of deep restful awareness. This is the state of deep meditation when your brain functions at the theta level but you are not asleep. At this stage you experience deep inner peace.

Beyond these three levels, there is a state, which is the highest level of relaxation and highest level of awareness. It contains both the delta and the gamma waves. It is the state of super consciousness or *Samadhi,* when the mind is completely absorbed. This is a state of pure bliss. It is when bliss happens irrespective of any external stimulus. The most wonderfully developed human nervous system is meant to experience this highest bliss, bliss uncaused by anything, bliss that is the very nature of your being.

Beyond this state, there is the state of pure consciousness where consciousness is crystal- clear. Not a bubble of any image, thought or imagination is left on consciousness. Mind stops working. Nothing exists except the deep awareness of pure being. This state is variously described as *Nirvana*, no-mind, *Satori, Buddha nature* or '*nirvikalpa Samadhi'*. No scientific device, so far, has been able to capture this supreme state of pure peace. Science lies way behind to capture this state of pure consciousness and explain it in terms of any numerical interpretation because this state of consciousness completely transcends the body which is the sole object of observation for the scientists. However, when you return from this state to normal state of consciousness you become a God-being. It is the zenith of all human experiences on earth.

PART II

OM AND LIFESTYLE

Om Chanting for Stress Relief

Stress is a normal part of modern life. However, too much stress is harmful. Stress causes insomnia, multiple sclerosis, diabetes, hypertension and many other health problems. Stress is often defined as the body's reaction to the emotional, mental or physical distress. This is a circular definition because stress is a circular phenomenon.

Cortisol is the main stress hormones created in the body. When the stress hormones are more than the normal, then we feel depressed and exhausted. Stress is a fight or flight response of the sympathetic nervous system (SNS). Systematic Om chanting and meditation produce relaxation response in the parasympathetic nervous system (PNS). Om chanting brings back the dominance of PNS over SNS and re-institutes the metabolic equilibrium in the body. Hypothalamic-pituitary-adrenal (HPA) axis is the multi-step biochemical pathway, which is responsible for maintaining the stress response of the body. This HPA axis is also known as the stress circuit of the body. Over activity of the HPA axis activities causes chronic stress.

Om meditation influences the Dorso-lateral prefrontal cortex and the limbic system in the brain in a balanced manner. Om Chanting significantly deactivates various regions of the brain, which are responsible for stress, strain and anxiety. Especially it deactivates the right amygdala. Over-reactive amygdala is the main center in the brain, which generates stress. Om chanting deactivates that area. Reverberation of the subtle vibration of soft humming Om produces relaxation response throughout the body. During the chanting we should rotate our awareness throughout the body in different paths. Stress relief is achieved, when energy is evenly distributed in the body. Om chanting with proper devotion and intention is the key component to move the vital energy in desired channels. Especially, movement of awareness along the spinal cord and the back portion of the body are vital. Visualize and feel the full body as the homogeneous light of Om. This visualization purifies many layers of the mind and liberates it from stress.

Om is continuously happening in your heart, in your breath. It is whispering in your soul. It is whispering in your blood. It is whispering in your cells. Om meditation is just listening to that silent melody of the life energy. If you want to conquer the anxiety of life, live in the moment, live in the breath.

Om as Silent Prayer

When you can not depend on your own strength, rely on the Om, the universal power of Love. This universal power of Love is not a male, nor a female. You can call Him or Her in any name; God, Iswara, Inner Light, Dhamma or Om. You can call it as the Holy Father or the Divine Mother. It does not matter. However, what matters is getting connected and staying connected with this universal force. The easiest way to get in touch with this universal power is through silent prayer. Listening to the inner Om chanting is the easiest way to bypass the chattering mind. Through prayer, you became one in love with that universal Love. Gradually you will realize that praying to the Om is loving the Om. Perfect prayer does not consist in many words. Silent remembering and pure intention raises the heart to that supreme power. Shut your eyes, shut your mouth, and open your heart. This is the golden rule of prayer. Prayer should be soundless words coming forth from the center of your heart filled with love. Offer your praise and gratitude to that universal Love with the whole of your heart and soul. Let the love of that universal force take complete and absolute ownership of your heart.

In meditation penetrate deep into the word “Om”. Gradually the word will disappear and only the silence will remain. The word is a support the meaning is within you. Om brings out that meaning which is hidden in your soul. Om is a living phenomena and every living thing has mood. Depending on its mood the wisdom will be revealed. Silence is the language of Om. We need to be silent to be able to reach our Self. Both internal and external silence is very important to feel the presence of that supreme Love. In silence, we can find new energy and true harmony. We should listen in silence, because if our heart is full of with other things we can not listen to the voice of that eternal Love. Great sages of all ages and religions have sought that great Truth, remaining in the silence and solitude for some time. Jesus, Ramana Maharshi, Buddha, Mohammad, Kabir and many saints spent few years of their life in silence and solitude to feel the presence of that eternal Love. We too often need to withdraw at certain intervals into the deeper silence and aloneness with that universal Love. We too need to be alone with Om. Not with our books, thoughts or memories but with a silent prayerful heart, we should lovingly dwell in solitude in the presence of Om. It is not a matter of doing; it is being in its purity that allows the Supreme Being to live within us. We need silence to listen what that eternal Being says to us. In silence, we feel oneness with the Universe. This feeling of oneness with the Universe gives us tremendous energy to overcome the problems of life and the fear of death.

Surrendering to Om

In surrender, we realize that we are nothing and in that nothingness, in that emptiness, the Divine power fills us with itself. Then from the fullness of that Love in our heart, we can do our work. Surrender does not mean carelessness. It means to be more careful; more careful about the presence of the divine Power of Om and love in each of our actions and in each aspect of our lives. Surrender does not mean laziness. Surrender does not mean negligence of duty. In fact, it is just the opposite. We have to do work in the spirit of love towards all and that love makes us perfect.

Om is the whole. Surrendering to Om means loving the Whole in its totality as it is. What matters is the degree of love that you put into each one of your action. That love is love towards Om. When that universal love sprouts in your heart, your surrender becomes complete and total.

Equanimity and Om Meditation

Equanimity does not mean sitting around inactive while things are happening, or escaping from the world, or suppressing one's feelings. Equanimity is operating from the state of supreme watchfulness without an iota of attachment or aversion. That is operating from the state of detached observer. Normally, like a wave, life continually moves between contrasts: success and failure, loss and gain, honor and blame, rise and fall. Usually, mind fluctuates with these waves. Equanimity means living above this fluctuating mind. Equanimity arises out of limitless love, compassion, and sympathetic joy towards the Whole existence, that we call Om.

Though it is very easy to say that one should observe the equanimity of mind, but in practice, it is very difficult to attain it because our mental faculty is always in grip of attachment and aversion. We can easily suppress, oppress or repress our mind and fool ourselves to believe that we are in equanimity. Nevertheless, that is not a state of equanimity, but a state of inertia. A mind of equanimity is an original pure mind free from all suppression, fear, anger, dullness and ignorance. Equanimity needs proper understanding of real nature of one's own Self as well as of others. The realization of the Self is only possible through equanimity and equanimity is only possible through the meditation of one's own real nature. The purpose of Om meditation is to realize that purest form of our real nature.

Sage Patanjali in his Yoga Sutra shows the way to culture equanimity in all situations of life. He prescribed that the mind becomes purified by cultivating feelings of friendliness towards those who are happy, compassion for those who are suffering, goodwill towards those who are virtuous, and indifference or neutrality towards those whom we perceive as wicked. These four behavioural cultivations are the foundation of Om meditation.

Practicing Om with other Mantras

Om means "yes"; it is a mantra of approval. Om is multiplier. If you are saying Om before any word, you are asking your inner self to give approval for that. As Om is a multiplier, when we say "Om peace", we are giving approval to increase peace vibration in the environment. Hence, we must be careful about using the Om mantra. We must always use Om mantra with auspiciousness, happiness, joy and Divinity.

Om is a pure word. We must utter "Om" with pure tongue. To get the benefit of the Om mantra, we must watch our tongues. We must use words that bring benefits to us and others. We must be careful before speaking.

Ruthless words and careless talks should be avoided, while one undertakes the practice of Om.

Om should not be used with any dead person's name because no human being, however noble, is free from faults, and the mental and physical defilements of that person may manifest within the worshipper as well as in the environment.

The Sanskrit word 'Shanti' means peace. Om is often used as "Om Shanti, Shanti, Shanti" which means "Let there be peace, peace and peace. This is a good mantra as it is associated with a good idea.

Om in Religions

The highest level of consciousness, "Om" encompasses all the religions. The most ancient texts of meditation Upanishads declared it as "Om" or "AUM". The Hindus as well as the Tibetan Buddhists adore it. It is called "Onkar" or "Ongkar" in Sikhism. It is "AMIN" for the Moslems; and "AMEN" for the Christians, Egyptians, Greeks, Romans and Jews. The seed syllable "Om" is used by the followers of Jainism as well. In Buddhism, "Om Mani Padme Hum" is one of the great mantras practiced by the Tibetan Buddhists. The Bible declares, "In the beginning was the Word and the Word was with God and the Word was God, and the word became manifest." The statement implies that the universe is nothing but an expression and manifestation of the Divine Vibration.

In Sikhism the "Mool mantra" or the root mantra is *"Ek Ong-kar Satnam Karta Purakh Nirbhau Nirvair Akal Murat, Ajuni Saibhang Gurprasad".* The meaning is as follows:

- EK ONG-KAR - There is only one God, its name is 'OM' or 'Ong-kar'. Ong-kar means the divine name of Om, also pronounced as Ong.
- SATNAM – It is the name of the truth.
- KARTA PURKH - It is the creator, which resides within..
- NIRBHAU - It is without fear.
- NIRVAIR - It is without hatred and without enemy.
- AKAAL MURAT – It is beyond time.
- AJUNEE SAIBANG - It is beyond birth and death and it is self-illuminating.
- GURU PARSAAD - It is the grace of the Supreme Truth..

Om is profusely praised in the Guru Granth Sahib Ji, the main religious scripture of the Shikhs in the following manner.

“This Shabad (word or sound) permeates the nucleus of the self, deep within, in its own home; the Light of this Shabad pervades the three worlds.”[Sri Guru Granth Sahib Ji]

“My attachment to Maya has been eradicated; the moon energy has devoured the Sun energy and then the un-struck sound current began to vibrate within.” – [Sri Guru Granth Sahib Ji]

PART III

OM MEDITATION

Om Meditation

Meditation on the Om has been a familiar and popular practice cultivated through centuries in the yoga tradition of India since the days of the Upanishads. This practice has proven to have tremendous benefits on the psyche of a human being. Om chanting is happening all the time in our body, in the nerves, in the spinal cord and in the brain. By exploring the Om inside the body, we can discover and transform our subconscious mind. By transforming our subconscious mind, we can realize our higher Self, the true nature. Meditation is resting at the inner core with supreme awareness.

Meditation on Om is the supreme meditation. There is nothing above that. Love of Om is the supreme love. Awareness of Om is the supreme awareness. Protection of Om is the supreme protection. Support of Om is the supreme support. Om is the highest God. Sound of Om is the supreme word of God. It is the supreme freedom, supreme openness, and supreme celebration. It is the supreme abode. It is the supreme refuge.

I have seen Om meditation quietly transforming and enriching the lives of individuals who undertook it with sincerity and devotion. I have seen it working miracles among the yoga students, to enhance their concentration, skill and performance. There were many who got relief from physical pain and discomforts. The protecting power of Om has brought emotional stability and mental poise in many of them. It has served as a dear friend when one was going through a time of crisis in his life. In the following pages, I have discussed a few techniques helpful for meditation with the sacred Om. When practiced regularly for ten to fifteen minutes a day, it can have a profound positive effect on our mental, emotional and physical health and wellbeing. However, if you feel any conspicuous physical or mental discomfort during any meditation, discontinue the practice and seek expert guidance. These meditations can be practiced any time during the day but it is important to have an empty stomach and remain unmoving for at least fifteen minutes after the session is over. The Meditations:

- Earth Touching Om meditation
- Cosmic Breathing Om meditation
- Meditation on the Luminous Sun of Om
- The Bow of Om: From Sounds to Silence
- Melting and Dissolving in the Ocean of Om
- Scanning the Body with Om
- Chakra Cleansing with Om
- Healing with Om
- Entering the Light of Om
- Walking with Om
- Gazing at Om

The Earth Touching Om Meditation

This is a practice to ground your energy body, connecting it with the earth. It can be practiced in the comfort of your home, though the best place to practice this meditation is a garden or a park or somewhere close to a natural setting.

The posture: Sit upright on a chair or a bench. The spine should be straight but supple and relaxed. Place your feet flat on the floor and slightly apart from each other. You may keep your hands cupped in your lap or place the right palm on the left. Keep your head erect as if you are looking straight ahead. Be careful that you do not let your chin drop on to your chest or bend your spine, as they block the flow of the breath as well as the flow of energy during the meditation.

The meditation: Gently close your eyes and feel your feet on the earth. Visualize the green planet as the big sphere on which you are sitting as a tiny body. Mentally observe your body slowly, from the front, from the back, from the left, from the right, from the bottom and from the top. Try to see that the earth is spinning round its own axis singing the holy Om and moving at dizzying speed encircling the Sun. You do not feel anything of the dizzying speed and the movement, thanks to the force of gravitation that pulls your body towards the earth and securely keeps you bound to the earth without impairing your freedom of movement.

Gently intone the sound of soft, long Om, surrendering your bodily being to the earth and to its gravitation, the power of Om. Feel yourself enveloped by the aura of Om emitted from the earth as you mentally chant the Om. Feel as if your physical body is one with the earth.

Suddenly stop chanting and in deep silence feel the touch of the earth with your feet. How does it feel beneath your feet- soft or hard, smooth or rough, wet or dry? Deeply feel the earth, knowing that it is absorbing all the negative energies from your body and mind and sending positive life-giving energies to keep you healthy, happy and balanced.

Before you finish, silently say Om as thanks in gratitude towards the mother earth that builds our body, nourish and sustain it, and holds us in its loving embrace.

Gently open your eyes and sit silently for a few moments absorbing the positive energy and peace of the environment.

Cosmic Breathing Om meditation

This is a practice to expand and unify your breath, connecting you with the cosmic breath. This meditation can be practiced in the comfort of your home or your balcony, though the best place to practice this meditation is under the open sky, in a garden or a park, or somewhere close to a natural setting.

The posture: Sit upright on a chair or a bench. The spine should be straight but supple and relaxed. Place your feet flat on the floor and slightly apart from each other. You may keep your hands cupped in your lap or place the right palm on the left. Keep your head erect as if you are looking straight ahead.

If you prefer traditional posture, you may sit in Lotus posture or half-Lotus on the ground on a blanket. However, take care that your spine stays straight and relaxed.

The meditation: Gently close your eyes and focus on your breaths as you breathe in and out in your natural rhythm. After you observe your natural pattern of breathing for a few moments, make your exhalation slow, deep and long, feeling that you are emptying yourself in to the Cosmos. Feel that you are being empty of everything, especially, of all the negative attributes of your body and the mind. Notice that immediately fresh air from outside rushes in to fill you with cosmic *Prana,* life force or the chi-energy. Inwardly say Om with the inhalation, feeling that you are inhaling the cosmic love, life, health and happiness.

Repeat this process of slow, long exhalation and the following deep inhalation uttering the Om. After some time be silent and come back to your natural breathing. Feel the energy-field within your body and remain silent as long as you like. You may lie down on your back if you like, keeping your legs apart and not crossed, to allow the energy to flow through your whole body.

Meditation on the Luminous Sun of Om

Sun is the living form of OM. The singing Sun, the singing moon, the singing stars and the singing galaxies are the direct expression of the divine word OM. Scientists believe that inside of the Sun rings like a bell. Sun is like a huge musical instrument. Meditate for a moment on how all life depends on the Sun. Om exists within us as the inner Sun of pure witnessing. It is the golden light of being that knows everything inside and outside of our body. To meditate on this inner Sun, sit quietly with the eyes gently closed. Feel your breath entering the nostril and going down to your heart, and then, coming up to go out of the nostrils. Be aware of this process for some time. Try to feel the breath, the warmth of it, as it flows.

Now, visualize the rising Sun in front of your face. Visualize the symbol of Om inside the Sun. Feel that it is entering within you with the incoming breath and going down to your heart. The Om settles there within your heart. Meditate on the light of Om in the heart center as if it is like a candle flame similar to the size of your thumb. Continue to see and feel the Sun within you. After some time, feel the golden orb of the Om is spreading until it covers all your limbs. Feel that the orb envelops your body and continues to expand until it holds the whole universe within it. The Sun of Om within your heart is at the center of this universe. You are the center of the universe. Extend your love, prayer and good will to all the beings of the entire universe. This meditation has unlimited potential to expand your consciousness, to awaken the higher Self within you.

Bow of Om: From Sounds to Silence

This practice helps you to silence the chattering mind creating calm and poise within you. This meditation can be practiced in the comfort of your home, at a place free from noises and external disturbances.

The posture: Sit upright on a chair. The spine should be straight but supple and relaxed. Place your feet flat on the floor and slightly apart from each other. You may keep your hands cupped in your lap or place the right palm on the left. Keep your head erect as if you are looking straight ahead.

If you prefer traditional posture, you may sit in Lotus posture or half-Lotus on the ground on a blanket. Take care that your spine stays straight, supple and relaxed. You may keep your hands on your knees.

The meditation: Gently close your eyes and focus on your breaths as you breathe in and out in your natural rhythm. After you observe your natural pattern of breathing for a few moments, softly utter long Om with the outgoing breaths, like O-o-o-o-M-m-m-m. . .

Keep your breathing natural. Now focus all your awareness on the sound of Om, as you utter it. Do it for some time and then, focus your attention on the silence after the utterance of Om ends.

After some time drop the chanting and feel only the silence. Feel your breathing, your body and your being absorbed in the silence. Be the Silence.

Before you finish, become aware of the sounds in your surrounding and gently open your eyes.

Dissolving in the Ocean of Om

This practice helps you to connect with the cosmic ocean of indestructible life energy from which all the beings are born and in to which they return after death. As a wave is part of the ocean, we all are indivisible part of this ocean of existence. There is no coming and going in reality; only transformation of form takes place as the wave becomes one with the ocean, as it melts and dissolves in to it. This meditation practice can give you a glimpse of your indestructible Self, removing the fear of death. It can be practiced at a secluded place that is free from noises and external disturbances.

The posture: Sit upright on a chair. The spine should be straight but supple and relaxed. Place your feet flat on the floor and slightly apart from each other. You may keep your hands cupped in your lap or place the right palm on the left. Keep your head erect as if you are looking straight ahead.

If you prefer traditional posture, you may sit in Lotus posture or half-Lotus on the ground on a blanket. Take care that your spine stays straight, supple and relaxed. You may keep your hands on your knees.

The meditation: Gently close your eyes and focus on your breaths as you breathe in and out in your natural rhythm. Now visualize a deep blue ocean around you. This is the cosmic ocean of oneness, which is the repository of love, life, abundance and all goodness of life. The ocean is deep and calm, with small waves here and there. You are a wave in this ocean. Now softly utter Om as you find yourself floating on the ocean. Hear your own uttering of soft Om, one after another, as the roaring of the ocean.

Do it as long as you like. Then utter a long Om and at the end of the utterance sink in the silence to be one with the ocean.

Remain silent as long as you can. Then be aware of your physical body, of the sounds of your environment and gently open your eyes.

Scanning the Body with Om

This practice helps you to connect with your body and increase self-awareness. Om is the cosmic life force. As the attention flows with Om, the cosmic *Prana* flows in the respective organs, nourishing and revitalizing them.

Throughout the day's activities, the mind is constantly active in thinking which makes the body exposed to stress. When we are under stress, we instinctively tense our muscles as part of 'fight-or-flight' response. We unconsciously transfer the tension to our muscles. This can affect the nervous system, the muscles and the health in general, in the long run, if you do not learn to consciously relax and release the pressure.

The following meditation practice can relax the body deeply by automatically silencing your thoughts. This practice is particularly effective when practiced in bed last thing at night and first thing in the morning to tone the body in preparation for the day ahead.

The posture: Sit upright on a chair. The spine should be straight but supple and relaxed. Place your feet flat on the floor and slightly apart from each other. You may keep your hands cupped in your lap or place the right palm on the left. Keep your head erect as if you are looking straight ahead.

The meditation: Gently close your eyes and become aware of weight of your body. Begin with a slow deep exhalation to expel all the stale air from your lungs. Repeat it for a few times. Now focus on your breaths as you breathe in and out in your natural rhythm. Mentally observe your body slowly, from the front, from the back, from the left, from the right, from the bottom and from the top.

Now visualize a ball of white light above the crown of your head. Gently intone Om and find the ball growing brighter and brighter. Gently focus on the top of your skull. As you softly intone Om, feel that the ball of light enters your head and the soft warm light spreading gently massaging your skull and the brain. With the next intonations of Om focus on your forehead, on your cheek, nostrils, ears and chin; and feel the light of Om flowing there to scan the area. Next, focus on the throat area, and with the soft intonation of Om, scan the area with the light. In this way go down through your chest, abdomen, and waist, and scan those areas with the light of Om with soft inward chanting.

Go down scanning through your right and left leg to reach the soles of your feet and then move your attention upward to come to the bottom of your spine. Now take a slow, deep breath, and as you exhale, inwardly chant a long, soft Om. Simultaneously, visualize the light of Om moving upward through the spine to gradually reach the top of your head and go out.

Now stop chanting and feel your whole body vibrant with the energy of Om. Move your attention from top of your skull to forehead, throat, chest, abdomen and ultimately to the sole of your feet to ground the energy.

Note: Grounding the energy to the earth is absolutely necessary for balance and stability in your body and mind. Never finish before you ground the energy by holding your attention to the sole of your feet.

Chakra Balancing with Om

The ancient yogis believed that there are seven major energy wheels or vortexes within our body. These psychic energy centers are imagined as spinning wheels of various colors.

During times of stress, the chakras can become drained of energy and it disrupts the free flow of life energy through them. These chakras are also disturbed as they become over or under-active due to wrong posture, lifestyle or exposure to tension. This causes an imbalance in the energy field in the body, which creates diseases.

The following meditation helps to attune, cleanse and energize the chakras in your body creating a sense of well-being within you.

Posture: Sit on the floor or on a chair with a straight back and keep your arms on your knees with palms upward. If you are sitting on a chair, place your feet flat on the floor.

The meditation: Gently close your eyes and slowly and deeply exhale expelling the stale air from your lungs. Now visualize a sphere of red light at the base of your spine. This chakra is your connection with the earth. Softly chant Om a few times, as you find the light becoming brighter and spreading horizontally and vertically below your seat to ground you in the earth.

Next visualize a sphere of soft orange light emerging at your Sacral chakra, approximately four inches below the navel. This is the light of your mind, when it is in a clear, peaceful and non-agitated state. Softly chant Om as you find the light shining brighter and spreading horizontally from back to the front. This light energizes your body and mind, and takes care of your physical and mental well-being. Note the feeling in this particular area of the body.

Next, visualize a third sphere made of golden yellow light at the Solar Plexus chakra, situated at your navel. This is the light of your intellect. The cosmic life force gathers here to spread all over your body. Softly chant Om as you find the light spreading and energizing this chakra. Take note of the feelings in this area.

Next, visualize a sphere of green light at your Heart chakra. Green is the color of life, love and Nature. Softly chant Om as you feel the light spreading to stimulate life energy within you. Note the feelings in your heart.

Next, visualize a ball of vivid blue light in your throat chakra. This light governs your speech and expression. Softly chant Om as you find the light glowing brighter and spreading to energize this area. Feel it.

Now visualize a sphere of light at your forehead at the middle of your eyebrows. Its color is indigo and it governs the faculty of intuition and wisdom. Softly chant

Om and see the light growing brighter. Feel the sensation in this area.

Finally, focus on the crown chakra at the top of your head and visualize a ball of white light with soft violet tinge in it. This light is your cosmic connection; it connects you with your higher Self. Remain absolutely silent as you find this light growing above your head to finally spread in to the universe.

After remaining at this stage of silent union with the cosmos for some time, bring back your attention to your body. Move your attention from top of your head to the eyebrow-center, from there to the throat center and further below, until you reach the bottom of your spine. Find all the spheres of light perfectly aligned along the axis of your spine and feel that they are attuned to one another, with the light of one chakra mixing and merging with another.

Watch the rainbow within your body as the body disappears in to the lights that melts and merges in to one another and streams upwards to form a fountain of pure white light above the Crown chakra.

When you are ready, gradually bring your awareness back to your body. Feel the air. Listen to the sounds in the environment and gently open your eyes.

Healing with Om

All the Om meditations discussed above have certain healing effects on the body and the mind. Om Meditation is a simple and effective way to cure many common ailments, particularly those that may be of a psychosomatic nature. This meditation helps you to align with the universal life force to regenerate the cells in your body and stimulate the body's natural defense mechanism

The posture: Sit upright on a chair. The spine should be straight but supple and relaxed. Place your feet flat on the floor and slightly apart from each other. You may keep your hands cupped in your lap or place the right palm on the left. Keep your head erect as if you are looking straight ahead.

If you prefer traditional posture, you may sit in Lotus posture or half-Lotus on the ground on a blanket. Take care that your spine stays straight, supple and relaxed. You may keep your hands on your knees.

The meditation: Gently close your eyes and focus on your breaths as you breathe in and out in your natural rhythm. Mentally observe your body slowly, from the front, from the back, from the left, from the right, from the bottom and from the top.

Now begin by visualizing a soft white ball of light above your head. Draw it down through the crown as you contemplate on Om as the source of all light, love, health, healing and vitality. Sense the cool touch of this pure light of Om penetrating and suffusing every cell of your brain. Next, visualize the light taking the form of a stream flowing down your body to cover your entire physical being, and forming an aura of white mist surrounding your body. Feel that this light is washing away all the impurities from every cell of your body. Sense this light of Om being absorbed in to every cell, saturating your bones, muscles, vital organs and the skin to spread out around your body as the mist.

Silently allow the light to caress, wash and purify your body, as long as you like. Then chant Om softly a few times, as you see the light withdrawing within your body. Gently open the eyes.

Entering the Light of Om

This meditation helps to heal and integrate your personality. It is best practiced in a secluded place in your home that is free from noise and disturbances. This visualization is used to reprogram the unconscious to dispel the negative conditionings, overcome fears and create a more positive attitude towards life in general.

Posture: Sit upright on a chair. The spine should be straight but supple and relaxed. Place your feet flat on the floor and slightly apart from each other. You may keep your hands cupped on your lap or place the right palm on the left. Keep your head erect as if you are looking straight ahead.

If you prefer traditional posture, you may sit in Lotus posture or half-Lotus on the ground on a blanket. Take care that your spine stays straight, supple and relaxed. You may keep your hands on your knees.

The meditation: Make yourself comfortable and gently close your eyes. Focus on your breath. Now visualize a ball of white light just in front of you, a few inches apart. This is the protective, nurturing light of Om. Within this light resides your higher Self, the eternal friend, philosopher and guide.

Keep softly gazing at the light as you find it drawing nearer and growing larger and brighter. See it growing bigger and bigger. When the light is about to touch your body, it has grown sufficiently large that you may enter the light. This light is cool, peaceful and you feel calm and serene as you come in to the contact with it. As you decide to enter the light this light becomes softer and larger to envelop you within it.

Stay within this light as you feel more centered, protected and in a state of Grace. Many symbols from the unconscious may come with this practice. As you are ready to finish, feel that the light becomes smaller and take the shape of your body, surrounding it. Become aware of the sensations within your body and gently open your eyes.

Walking with Om

Contrary to the popular notion, meditation is not solely concerned with sitting in silence with the eyes closed. One of its primary objectives is to open our minds to a greater reality in which we become aware of our cosmic connection; we become aware that we share an interconnected existence with all the beings and things in the universe and our apparent sense of separation is an illusion.

There are many techniques of meditations that are practiced with the eyes open. The Om walking meditation is one of such techniques. The best places for this practice are the parks and the gardens, though one can practice it on the pavements of a road that is solitary and free from the traffics.

Posture: Stand upright with spine straight but relaxed. Lift your chin to look straight forward. Keep your hands loosely hanging down the sides of your body.

The meditation: Before you begin, take a deep breath. Inhale and exhale deeply. Look at the surroundings. Feel the wind blowing, hear the birds chirping, or take note of any other sights or sounds in your environment. Now begin by being alert of your posture. Make a mental note of the sensations in the body.

Now begin to walk slowly, taking each step consciously. Become aware of the movement of your feet. Become aware as they touch the ground. When you enter a rhythm, turn your attention to your breath. Count your breath with short Om as you breathe in and out, naturally. Find the natural ratio of your in-breath and out-breath. Is it a 3:4 ratio, or is it 2:3? Whatever be your ratio do not try to alter it. Once you find your ratio, count the outgoing breaths with Om. For example, if you have a 3:4 breathing ratio, mentally say Om four times with the outgoing breath. Remain silent as you breathe in. Keep on breathing and walking in a relaxed manner. Do not speed up or slow down too much. Walk for ten to fifteen minutes at your convenience. This is a wonderful exercise in concentration and awareness. It will help to integrate all the layers of your being.

Gazing at Om

This meditation practice brings a heightened sense of awareness as it sharpens the faculty of concentration. It may help to develop self-discipline, cultivate self-confidence and improve personal performance in sports and business.

A plain background like a wall without decoration is needed for this purpose. Keep the symbol of Om ॐ on the wall. Alternatively, you may light a candle, place it in front of the wall and gaze at the candle flame, as the flame is a symbol of the light of Om.

The posture: Sit upright on a chair or on the floor. Place the object of your meditation at the same level of your eyes. The spine should be straight but supple and relaxed. Place your feet flat on the floor and slightly apart from each other, if you sit on a chair. You may keep your hands cupped in your lap or place the right palm on the left. Keep your head erect as you are looking straight ahead. Be careful that you do not let your chin drop on to your chest or bend your spine, as they block the flow of energy during the meditation.

The meditation: Gently focus on your breath. Notice how the air is flowing in and out of your nostrils. Be very still but relaxed. Now softly gaze at the Om or at the flame of the candle. Do not judge or study the object. Simply stare at it without blinking much. Do not strain your eyes. If your eyes become watery, gently close them for a few moments and then again open your eyes and stare at the Om. Feel that a connection is being established between you and your object of observation. Notice the flow of your breath. See how still or slow they have become.

After ten to fifteen minutes, gently close your eyes. Find the image of Om within you. As you do so, you may feel that the distinction between you and Om has vanished. Do not judge or analyze the feeling. Just enjoy losing yourself in the Om.

After a period of silence bring back your awareness to your body and gently open the eyes.

PART IV

OM IN SCRIPTURES

Philosophy of Om

We are not separate beings in this universe. All are interconnected. Om is the mantra of integration; integration of individual with the Whole. Om is the mantra of harmony and celebration.

Indian spirituality and philosophy is impregnated with Om, which is widely mentioned in the Upanishads, Tantras and the Puranas. Om is mentioned in the Yajur Veda, where it is known as the ‘Pranava’, ‘the humming sound’ or ‘Udgita’, meaning, 'the elevating chant’. Ancient scriptures repeatedly mentioned Om as "Ek aksharam Brahman", which means Om is the monosyllable representing Supreme Truth. It is the non-dual supreme reality. Ancient scriptures extols the glory of Om as they say, 'Know it as the essence of purity, as the light of light.'

Although Om is the single letter supreme truth it is the entire existence, non-existence and the beyond. However, our mind is comfortable with plurality and divisions. Particularly, our brain is very comfortable with three objects or things at a time. So, to make it easy for the mind to grasp the vastness of the Om mantra, the ancient sages and seers taught us to see the Om mantra as a combination of three letters A,U,M and the silence. To grasp the vastness of the Om and to express the multidimensional aspect of the Om, these three letters A, U and M are given along with different interpretations. They associated the letters A,U, M with different levels of our consciousness.

The most fundamental philosophy of the Om mantra as declared in Mandukya Upanishad is "Ayam Atma Brahman", which means there is no difference between the individual self, 'I am' and the cosmic Self, the Whole. According to this scripture, both at the individual and the cosmic level, the Self has four states, namely, waking, dreaming, deep-sleep and the Turiya which is the transcendental, deep-silence of the pure Self. The letters of A, U, M and the silence following its utterance denotes these four states of consciousness, both at the individual and cosmic level.

There is no difference between the waking state and the dream state. The objects of the waking state are as unreal as the objects of the dream state. Deep silence denoted by complete absence of thought is our true nature; it is the state of infinite bliss. It is the state of formless and timeless awareness. Om chanting and Om meditation is the way and means to keep your focus on the present moment, connecting you with the absolute truth of your being.

Mandukya Upanishad

Mandukya Upanishad is the essence of all Upanishads and Vedas. Mandukya Upanishad describes the essence of Om. It has twelve verses. Meditation on these twelve verses alone is sufficient for any aspirant to get liberation. It is the direct path for realizing oneness with the universe, the Whole. It is the way to unite the individual personality with the universal Self. It is the way to tune the individual rhythm with the cosmic rhythm. Each utterance of Om, connects us to our ultimate cosmic personality. It is the means to dissolve the individual ego into the cosmic Self. It is also the way to operate through the pure all auspicious cosmic consciousness, which is our true nature. An enlightened man is the one who flows with the Whole. Om is the way and the goal to flow with the Whole.

The Verses of Mandukya

1) Hari Om. The soundless sound Om is all this. All that is past present and future is the soundless sound Om. That which is beyond the three periods of time is also, indeed, the soundless sound Om.

2) All of this, everything, everywhere, is the Absolute Truth Om. Our very Self is the Absolute Truth Om. Our Cosmic Self has four states through which it operates.

3) The first state of the Cosmic Self is the Waking state, where the consciousness is turned outward to the external world of objects. Through its seven instruments and nineteen channels, it enjoys the gross objects of the world.

Note:

[Cosmic Self operates through the nineteen channels of the individual personality. They are: Five organs of perception + Five organs of action + Five aspects of Vital energy + Mind + Intellect + Ego + Memory.

Seven Instruments of Cosmic Self= Infinite Space + All Life Forces + Matters + Water + Energy + Air + Cosmic Rules]

4) The second state of the Cosmic Self is the Dream state. In this state, consciousness is turned towards the inner world. It also operates through seven instruments and nineteen channels, which enjoys the subtle objects of the mental world.

5) The third state of the Cosmic Self is the Deep Sleep. In this state, there is neither the desire for any gross or subtle object, nor any dream. In deep sleep, all such experiences have merged into the ground of undifferentiated consciousness. The entire consciousness is full of bliss and it is the enjoyer of bliss, and it is the gateway into the other two preceding states; the dream and the waking state.

6) This Cosmic Self of the deep sleep state is the Lord of all, this is the knower of all, this is the inner controller of all beings, and this is the womb, out of which all of the other beings emerge. All things originate from and dissolve back into this source.

7) The fourth state of the Cosmic Self is Turiya, which means beyond the three. In this state, consciousness is neither turned outward nor inward. Nor is it both outward and inward; it is beyond both cognition and the absence of cognition. It can not be experienced through the sense organs. It is beyond comparison, deductive reasoning or inference. It is indescribable, incomprehensible, and unthinkable by the mind. This is Pure Consciousness itself. This is the real Self. It is within the cessation of all phenomena. It is peaceful, auspicious and non-dual. This is the real or true Self that is to be realized.

8) The Cosmic self, though described as having four states, is indivisible; it is pure Consciousness itself. That Consciousness is Om. The three sounds A-U-M and the three letters A, U, M are identical with the three states of waking, dreaming, and deep sleep, and these three states are identical with the three sounds and letters.

9) The Sound "A" represents the waking state of the Cosmic Self and A, is the first letter of Om. That simple sound of A is first and permeates all other sounds. One who is aware of this first level of reality has fulfillment of all desires and becomes the first or the foremost among all.

10) The Sound "U" represents the Dream state of the Cosmic Self and U, is the second letter of Om. This intermediate state operates between the waking and sleeping states, reflecting some qualities of the other two. One who is aware of this subtler state is superior to others. For one who is aware of this state, the knower of Absolute truth will be born into his family.

11) The Sound "M" represents the Deep sleep state of the Cosmic Self and M, is the third letter of Om. It contains the other two, and is that from which the other two emerge, and into they recede or merge. One who is aware of this state of cosmic Self is able to know the real nature

of the things and being, and he comes to realize the Self of all.

12) Pure Silence is the fourth state of the Cosmic Self. It is the soundless sound aspect of Om. It is not utterable and is not comprehended through the senses or by the mind. It is cessation of all phenomena, all blissful and non-dual. This fourth state is the real Cosmic Self. One, who is aware of this state, merges his self into the Supreme Cosmic Self the Universal Consciousness.

Footnote: A, U, M and the silence thereafter, represents four different states of our consciousness. These states of consciousness are closely related to how our brain waves function. The relation between the four levels of consciousness and our brain waves are discussed in the levels of consciousness section.

Om in Patanjali's Yoga Sutra

In Patanjali Yoga Sutra, the most scientific and ancient yoga tradition (around 1000 - 800 B.C.), Om is hailed as the goal, means as well as the way to reach the supreme reality. In this ancient yoga treatise, there are three verses, which describe the importance of Om for Self-realization. The verses are as follows:

"Om is the sound that symbolizes the supreme truth." [1.27]

"One should chant Om remembering its true meaning." [1.28]

"By chanting and meditating on this Om, one will realize the Self within and all the obstacles will be removed". [1.29]

Om in the Bhagavad-Gita

"O Arjuna, I am the taste of pure water, and the light of the moon and the sun. I am the essential nature of the mantra Om mentioned in the Holy Scriptures, the sound in ether, as well as the courage and virility of human beings."[7.8]

"Whoever intones Om, knowing it as representing Brahman, and thinks of Me when his soul leaves the body, that person shall attain the supreme goal." [8.13]

"I am the sum of all knowledge, the sacred syllable Om". [9.17]

"Among the words I am the monosyllable Om". [10.25]

"Those who follow the Vedas, always repeat the word Om before offering sacrifices, giving gifts and performing spiritual practices." [17.24]

Om in Katha Upanishad

"The goal which all the Vedas declare, which all austerities aim at, and which men desire when they lead the life of celibacy, I will tell you briefly: it is Om. This syllable Om is indeed Brahman. This syllable is the Highest. Whosoever knows this syllable obtains all that he desires. This is the best support; this is the highest support. Whosoever knows this support is adored in the world of Brahma." [Katha Upanishad 1.2.15-1.2.17]

Om in Mundaka Upanishad

"Taking the hold of thc bow, the great weapon of the Om, one should place in it the arrow of self sharpened by meditation. Drawing the string, O beloved, hit that very target, known as that Imperishable Brahman." [Mundaka Upanishad 2.2.3]

"Om is the bow; the individual self is the arrow; and Brahman is spoken as its target. It is to be hit without making a mistake. One should become one with it just like an arrow (becomes one with the target after hitting it)." [Mundaka Upanishad 2.2.4]

Om in Prashna Upanishad

"Anyone who meditates on the supreme Cosmic Self with the help of this very syllable Om, as possessed of three letters, becomes unified in the Sun, consisting of light. As a snake becomes freed from its dead skin, exactly in a similar way, he becomes freed from sin."[5.5]

"The enlightened man attains that (threefold) world through Om alone; and through Om as an aid, he reaches supreme Reality that is quiet and beyond old age, death and fear."[5.7]

Om in Chandogya Upanishad

"One should meditate on this Syllable Om." [Chandogya Upanishad 1.1.1]

"That is the quintessence of the essences, the supreme and the highest." [Chandogya Upanishad 1.1.3]

"Speech and breath are joined together in the Syllable Om." [Chandogya Upanishad 1.1.6]

"Meditate on the rays of the Sun as Om." [Chandogya Upanishad 1.5.2]

"The breath is continually resounding 'Om.' [Chandogya Upanishad 1.5.3]

"This is the Udgitha (the song as Om, which uplifts the singer), the most excellent; this is endless. He who, knowing this, meditates on the Udgitha obtains progressively the most excellent life and wins the most outstanding worlds." [Chandogya Upanishad 1.9.2]

Om in other Upanishads

"Om is Brahman. Om is all this. Om is the whole. Om is uttered to indicate consent. The priest begins worship with Om. Spiritual teachers begin their lessons with Om; and their disciples open themselves to those lessons with Om. He who utters Om with the intention 'I shall attain Brahman' does verily attain Brahman." (Taittiriya Upanishad 1.8.1-2)

"Just as the fire that is hidden in its source-material is unseen and yet remains latent, but can be generated from its source repeatedly by means of friction, so is the case with the self in this body, which has to be yoked by means of the syllable Om.

Using the body as the lower piece of the wood and the syllable Om as the upper friction rod, and practicing meditation as the act of friction, one can see God who is hidden in oneself. " [Svetasvatara Upanishad 1:13,14]

"One should duly practice concentration on Om (first) through the means of its letters, then meditate on Om without regard to its letters. Finally, on the realization with this latter form of meditation on Om, the idea of formlessness is realized.

That alone is Brahman, without components or parts, without doubt and without taint. Realizing 'I am that

Brahman' one becomes the immutable Brahman." - Amrita Bindu Upanishad [7-8].

"Om is the primordial throb of the universe. It is the sound form of Atma (Consciousness)." - Maitri Upanishad

"Let Om be the bow, mind the arrow, and Higher Consciousness the target. Those who want enlightenment should reflect on the sound and the meaning of Om. When the arrow is released from the bow it goes straight to the target." - Dhyana Bindu Upanishad [14, 15]

"The short (accent of OM) burns all sins, the long one is decayless and the bestower of prosperity. United with Ardha-Matra (half-metre of OM), the Pranava becomes the bestower of salvation." Dhyana Bindu Upanishad [17]

"One should contemplate upon Om as Ishvara resembling an unshaken light, as of the size of a thumb and as motionless in the middle of the lotus of the heart." Dhyana Bindu Upanishad [19]

"Making the mind the lower wood, and OM the upper wood, by the repeated friction of knowledge, a wise man burns up all the bonds." Kaivalya-upanishad [11].

“By sound one becomes liberated.” [Brahma Sutras 4.4.22]

Om in the Purana

The Shiva Purana states that recitation of Om purifies our mind and leads us automatically to salvation. The Narada Purana encourages the Yoga practitioner to fix Om in the heart center while meditating.

"Let him recite the Gayatri Mantra prefixed with the mystic syllable Om, mother of all the Vedic mantras"
Garuda Purana

"I pay respects to the Ineffable Intelligence which is symbolized by the sacred syllable Om."
- Bhagavat Purana

Salutation to Om

"Omkaram bindu samyuktam
nityam dhyayanti yoginah.
Kamadam mokshadam chaiva
Omkaraya namo namah"

"The yogis always meditate on the Om along with its bindu, the point of merging in to the silence. Salutation to the Om, who fulfills all desires and also bestows us the supreme state of liberation."

About the Author

Dr. Amit Ray is a teacher of meditation and spiritual development. He is author of several books on meditation and other spiritual topics. He learnt yoga and meditation from the masters of the ancient Himalayan Yoga and Buddhist traditions. He began sharing his experiences after a series of transformative spiritual awakening. In his Himalayan Centre at Uttarkashi, he lives a life dedicated to meditation and yoga.

In his early years, he was a scientist. He did his PhD in artificial intelligence and computational neuroscience and worked as a scientist in India, UK and USA. With a spiritual bent of mind from his very childhood, he undertook intense practices in meditation from his early years. In his later years, many mystical experiences prompted him to dedicate his life for the search of truth.

Acknowledgements

I express my humble respect and gratitude to all the sages, seers and teachers, both ancient and modern that helped me directly or indirectly, through their words, presence or teachings.

I express my gratitude to the team at the Inner Light Publishers for their tireless effort and enthusiasm. I would like to express my love and gratitude to all of my students and friends for their support and love.

I am moved by the efforts of all my meditation students in trying to understand and apply the teachings, and I pray to the Divine Om for their success.

Also from Inner Light Publishers

Yoga and Vipassana: An Integrated Lifestyle

Integrated Yoga and Vipassana meditation is a clear and straightforward guide to awaken the light within. For those who are interested in deep meditation to attain spiritual freedom and fulfillment in every sphere of life, this book is a practical and personal manual. ISBN: 9788191026924

Laughing Buddha: The Alchemy of Euphoric Living

The spirit of Laughing Buddha is the spirit of ultimate relaxation, happiness and contentment. This book gives a rare combination of ancient Buddhist wisdom and its practical use in our daily lives in the modern world for living in joy. ISBN: 9788191026948

We at Inner Light Publishers are dedicated to publishing books that helps improve the quality of human lives. You are welcome to visit us at www.inner-light-in.com.

27121966R00070

Printed in Great Britain
by Amazon